Butterflies

CHRONICLES OF A LOV

Syed Arslan Ali Zaidi

ISBN-10: 1717321224
ISBN-13: 978-1717321220

DEDICATION

To the ones I loved, and the ones that got away; to the ones that I lost, and the ones that I found; to the ones I gave hope to, and the ones that believed in me; to the ones that ache, and the ones that hold on; to the ones that are numb, and the ones that have moved on; I write this for you. You know that overwhelming void in your heart that feels like something is missing? There are thousands of black holes like those spread across the entire universe, from where another soul has travelled across the stars to find you. When that day comes, all the underlying forces in the universe will fall into place. In that moment, any such void shall cease to exist. What was meant to be will no longer need to find its way; it will have found home.

Email: ArslanWrites@Gmail.com
Facebook: www.Facebook.com/ArslanWrites
Instagram: @ArslanWrites
Website: www.ArslanWrites.com

Ordering Information: Quantity sales. Special discounts are available on quantity purchases by corporations, associations, and others. For details, contact the publisher via CreateSpace Direct.

Cover image: Lukas Gojda/Shutterstock.com
Interior Illustrations by:
DODOMO/Shutterstock.com
Valenty/Shutterstock.com
GN/Shutterstock.com
One line man/Shutterstock.com

ISBN-10: 1717321224
ISBN-13: 978-1717321220

First Edition

and
so
it
begins.

She was music
in a world
unacquainted
with sound.

Instagram: @ArslanWrites

With
a smile
like that,

the world
was hers
for the taking.

My heart
stood no
chance,

for it
was hers
at first
sight.

Rapt
in wonder
of you,

it is
beyond
me to
attain
any sense
of reality.

Unfathomable
is what it is,

whatever
your eyes
do to me.

And if you ever wonder,
in a sky full of stars you'd
be the moon;

more than a thousand
times enough.

And
perhaps
even the
stars look
down
at her
as if she's
all that
exists.

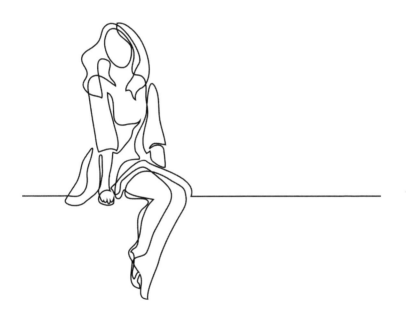

All hell broke loose;
and in the midst of it all,
I found paradise in you.

She was the definition of a force to be reckoned with, and I was all about colliding with whatever that had the potential to destroy me.

Instagram: @ArslanWrites

There sat next to me,
perfection;

and my God was she
beyond my wildest perception.

When she laughs,
my God it's like
a divine composition,

for if heaven were to sing,
it'd sound like her.

It's
only fair
isn't it?

For the
flashbacks
of all
the glimpses
that I
stole
of you,

to keep
me up
at night?

And
perhaps
the worst
of them all,

is the
feeling
of longing.

-    it never ends.

Slow down;
for you are
not meant to
chase anyone.

Darling,
have you ever
seen yourself?

You make
the winds fall
off course,

just to stay
in sync with you.

- a note to the reader

I've got a mind
full of perhaps
and maybes,

torn between
what ifs and
what could bes.

Oh how I wish
not to be consumed
by such uncertainties.

I've
noticed
time and
time again,

the distance
between bliss
and chaos
is only a
matter of
your presence.

She
had fallen
apart at the
hands of it;

but her
smile could
put the
world
together.

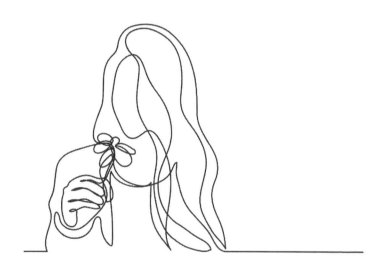

I've never found myself
in love ever so restlessly
from the moment I saw
the beauty of your unveiled face.

Ever since, night or day...
I've lost control of my gaze
as my eyes search for you endlessly.

There
are a
million
maybes
on my
mind.

Maybe this,
Maybe that.

Maybe,
now just
isn't the
right time.

Instagram: @ArslanWrites

Like the depths of the sea, there's more to you than I'll know with the passing of time. I'm interested beyond the shallow, in the deep dark bits of your mind. I want to know what controls your thermocline, and have your surface aggression dance with mine. I want to get lost in your depths and be engulfed by everything you find to be true. I want to be stranded and surrounded by nothing but you. I want to be the light that gets submerged so far into your soul that I become the only one to ever penetrate through the abyssopelagic of your core. I want to conquer your Hadal realm, and be named its King. I want to defeat all that haunts you at night, and claim your treasures as mine. I want to name you my ocean and raise hell upon all that looks to you. Every shipwreck will mark my territory of being the one that the seas took to be theirs. The seven seas are one in their entirety, a body of water that would be mine.

-   Poseidon

My
mind
is a maze.

Maybe
that's why
you cant
find your
way out
of it.

Destinations;
you've got yours
and I've got mine.

Perhaps it is naïve
to ask for the ends
of our paths to intertwine.

- knots

I'm in
love with
every corner
of this city,

because
at some
point you
may have
been there.

At some
point,

our
paths
will cross
again.

I'd
love you
to the ends
of the earth,

and off
the edge
I'd fall;

for you
all over
again.

Her
presence
is not only
illuminating
but it
aromatizes
her vicinity,

for the
fragrance
of a million
roses is
distilled
within her
soul.

Instagram: @ArslanWrites

It is as if every particle of her existence was a piece of the universe brought together as one. She was so much more than flesh and bones wrapped in velvet skin. She had the glow of the sun that refreshed the sight of those that saw her, she was the scent of a garden of perennials unforgettable to those she met, she was the star dust from a thousand stars collected over millennials that gave purpose to the night, her smile was the inverted arch of the sound waves created by the chanting of angels, her mood like the seasons that changed all for beautiful reasons, her grace and elegance the signature of womanhood, from her eyes to the very breath she takes has a purpose intrinsic to the universe, for it was a part of her.

Your heart is home to me.
I'll always be lost until
you find a way in for me.

It's as if my heart had a
compass which pointed to you,

and magically,
magnetically,
and oh so inevitably,
I was drawn to you.

Under a breath beneath the moon,
I whispered to her words I couldn't say.
She was oblivious to what she meant to me.
The heavens knew,
the angels knew,
but she could never see it.

Perhaps
you and I
were two
souls,

shot
through
the skies
to see if
we'd end
up finding
each other
in this
world.

  -   we did

The
most
exquisite
of spirits
fail to be
intoxicants
as potent
as your eyes;

any man
would cease
to have
control
over his
desire to
value its
elixir over
his own demise.

Instagram: @ArslanWrites

She
shared
the kind
of intimacy
with the night,

where a star
would dim
in the sky
for every
tear she
shed from
her eyes.

It
intrigued
me how
the epitome
of beauty
itself would be
awestruck
by nature,

for she
had an
admiration
for roses
similar to
the way
she took
my breath away.

Instagram: @ArslanWrites

The
absence
of light
can be a
beautiful thing.

Ask the
lonesome heart
that finds
comfort
in the
arms of a
sleepless night.

My
demons
were as
helpless
in front of her
as wolves
that howled
to the full moon.

There was
absolutely
no self-control,

as if
her
entirety
was a
magnet
to my soul.

Her
purities
are too
sacred to
contaminate,

as if
the hope
in tomorrow
would
die with it.

Show
me the
part of you
that's broken.

Your pieces
will fit
well with mine.

Don't
hide your
darkness,

I'm
sure
it'll light
up mine.

Instagram: @ArslanWrites

What do you call the
togetherness of two
souls in pending?

Have you ever wondered,
or is it just me?

You don't know me well enough,
but we'll get to that – eventually.
I just cant stand not knowing who you are.
You intrigue me like a mystery.
I want to know things about you
that no one would even ask,
like what would it take to light your fire,
exponentially?

I'm not just interested in a dance with your devil,
I want to know what drives it insane.
Introduce me to the demons that
you've fought with and slain.

Small talk doesn't concern me;
I'm interested in your flames.
We've all got a fire,
but yours I want to fuel.
Imagine clouds of gasoline pouring down your soul,
igniting passion far beyond your control.

Why make small talk when you can tell me about the turmoil within your soul? Tell me everything you love and all the things you hate. I know it's a little too early, but why wait till it's too late? Getting comfortable is just a social construct. I want you to say what comes to mind, with no need to be abrupt.

Your eyes clearly want to talk, and I feel like being attentive. You can go on forever, how's that for an incentive? What keeps you up at night? What monsters make you toss and turn in bed? Are there any mischievous rumors that you've spread? What instruments do you play, or what's the last book you've read? What's the funniest moment in your life, and what was the last song to get stuck in your head? Tell me something crazy about yourself that I wouldn't believe, and tell me all the tricks that you've got up your sleeve. Do you even believe in magic? How would you define tragic? What makes you smile, and what enrages you to the point you need to scream? Just look me in the eyes, and tell me who you are. Why be a stranger? I know way too many of those.

They
tried to
warn me
of her
hurricanes,

but
I was
the type
to embrace
hurricanes
with open arms.

Sure,
I was
reckless.

But
boy…
was she
worth the
calamity!

I'd be lying if I said she was a sky full of stars. She wasn't. In fact she was comprised of a series of constellations that spelled out a name, spread across entire galaxies. Her entirety was the phenomenal fusion of those galaxies molded into the existence of her being. Her eyes spoke of nothing but worlds that I'd often get lost looking in, and the sparkle in her gaze when she smiled was even more than celestial. There was a chasm full of bliss between her legs, almost like a stargate leading into an abyss of galaxies of her own. The glow on her face after being satisfied would outshine all the stars that glistened in the skies. She was the epitome of time and space. Her kiss would make me lose sense of gravity as if setting foot on ground was a concept never known to man. The sound of her voice would make my heart stop in serenity as if time itself was at a standstill. When she laughed, I wished the resumption of time had only been a myth for the sounds of her laughter were a cure for the wounds of nature herself. She healed as if she was the cure to everything ever missing inside of me as if I was nothing but stardust and her touch was meant to complete me into something within her orbit. Everything about her was interstellar, and even that was short of the truth.

I pray that the love you
claim to have healed you
isn't the same one that
destroys you in the end.

For I have learned that
your ultimate devastation
comes disguised as your savior.

- a note to the reader

If they were to ask me
what it is that I fell for,
I would say her entirety.
For there is not one thing
about her that I would
want differently.

Perhaps
you too
are unattainable,

like
the stars
and the moon
are out of
my reach.

The
flaws
in me
want to
acquaint
with the
flaws in
you,

and
simply
arouse them
into
perfection.

She is as much
mine, as I am hers;
a divine right.

What is written,
falls together
with time; she is
no one else's to take.

My heart gets caught in my throat,
At the thought of losing you.

There are some nights
which I don't want to end.
And of those nights are the
ones in which I have
all your attention;
the ones that make me
feel as if we're the only
ones in the world.

Instagram: @ArslanWrites

Our hearts might be an aphelion apart like the earth from the sun, but it is solely you that I revolve around. Like the magic between the earth and the moon, you unknowingly pull at me with all that you've got to bring me closer to you. My heart as rampant as water begins to disown me, for it is the one thing I have no control over and you control so uncontrollably. Tidal waves of emotions overwhelm me night and day as if it is predetermined, and self-control is only an illusion for it seems beyond me. It seems as if I, in my entirety do not belong to myself… for my soul is entrapped within my being, but it longs to be with you.

I'm beginning to enjoy
the company of
absolute loneliness,
for it is in this loneliness
I lose myself to the thought
of you for hours on end.

And perhaps what I want most is for you to know more than just the illusion of me. I want you to be able to look right through me and understand more than what I say; perhaps even the whispers of my soul in the silence between you and I. For you to be able to feel the battle scars on and within my being and know exactly the kinds of wars I've fought with and beyond my mind, as each will tell you more and more about the man that I am. I want you to know what I believe in, what I stand for, and what enrages me beyond madness. I want you to know what I'd die for, what I'd kill for, and how far I would go to protect what is mine. I want you to drown in the depths of me and conquer my storms and master my demons. I want to be yours and be accepted for all that I am, as much as I wish for you to be mine in all you entirety.

I whispered
my love for you
to the setting sun,

and my secret
illuminated the
other side of the world.

You are both,
my affliction
and its cure.

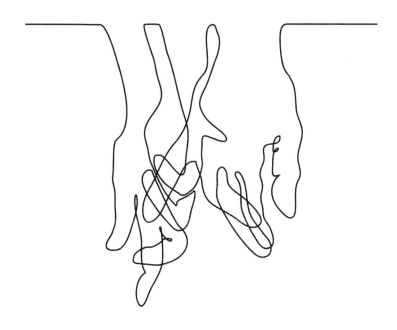

Like the waves that longed to subside with the shore, all I ever wanted was to collapse in your existence. The turbulence in my soul sought refuge, a thirst to be quenched only by your presence.

You may not believe in love,
but I know you to be true.
You my dear are love.

No matter
how deep
the tunnel,

just the
thought of
you is light.

If I could wake up next to you,
I'd pull you close and never let go.

The offset chance of it being a dream,
would be too big a chance to ever take.

She
built a
wall
around
her heart
to keep
everyone out,

I built
my home
around it,

and
asked
her to
let me
in.

Sanity
did not
intrigue me;

it was
the wildfire
in her soul
that had
mine up
in flames.

Someone once asked me what I'd steal if the whole world was asleep. I remember saying I would wait for the world to be awake so it would witness me taking what I want. I know what it is now. I would catch you off guard, and I would steal a kiss. Would you hold that against me?

If I could yell your name from the peak of the highest point in this world, I would take all that is below me as witness that it is you that I pray to the skies for. And if I could dive into the deepest ends of the earth, I would take all that is above me as witness that it is you that I have fallen for. But I am constricted to the realms between all that is above and below. So I will conquer it from corner to corner and tell every last soul, that it is you that I will slay it for, lest it decides to hurt you.

The expressions in her eyes are poems for me to decipher; for nothing is by chance as the universe has conspired for me to find her. Shot through the skies from a million light years away, my soul has travelled; for there are revelations encrypted within her soul that are specifically mine to unravel.

As much as I loved you,
I hated every single thing
that hurt you far more than
anything else.

I was a contaminant,
and you were pure.
I was abominable
and you were my cure.

I was hell
and you were all things divine.
I was your weakness
and you were mine.

Within me, I carried a storm. At times the winds became tempestuous and my mind was engulfed by hurricanes. I was always more beast than man, easily enraged, destructive, and untamable. At times I had no control of even myself, and to conquer the storms within me, I'd have to find ways to neutralize the intensities within myself. I'd look for anything that can help me self-destruct. I searched until what I was looking for ended up finding me instead. My hurricanes became mere thundershowers of mercy that poured at the sight of her big brown eyes, and in it I drowned mercifully in love. She domesticated the hurricanes that vowed to destroy me.

Love itself seems to be bipolar. If it has found you during its highs, I pray to the powers that be for you to never experience it at its low. And if you've caught it at its low, I pray that it changes for you so. For somewhere between the highs and lows of love, suffers its victim; an equilibrium that you know to be yourself that no longer remains as such. Adjusting to its propensities only leaves you numb. May you never have to be the one caught in the middle of its onslaught.

- a note to the reader

Perhaps what I fear most is that you'll give yourself a thousand excuses to why you think that I don't make sense in the way I feel for you, and those thousand excuses will become a thousand reasons to why you'll never feel the same, and it'll all inevitably become the thousands of ways you pushed me away. But to every time you fail to believe in us, I'll always have one thing to say. I believe enough for the both of us, and I know one day you'll see it my way.

Perhaps what intrigued me most about finding her broken was that I could fix her in any way that I wanted. She was shy of her pieces, but was mine to build on. And with every smile that I knew I had put on her, it felt as if I knew what I was doing when in fact, I didn't. In all honesty I had absolutely no idea. All I knew was that I had to make sure the new her would never succumb to the old one. The thought of having to be so much more than I was to make sure the past would never matter again, worried me. I had to be everything and more, when all I really knew was how to be myself. Every time the past came up, I reminded her that she was mine now. I knew if I loved her right, it would be enough to make her into ten times the woman she could have ever been without me. Her smile was definitely reassuring.

He complained of being made of fire as he pushed her away, being completely unaware that only she could have put him out. Like opposite ends of a spectrum, they were two extreme intensities. She had the power to neutralize him whenever he came close to the verge of burning the world to the ground. All it took was a touch of her lips against his, and his rage succumbed to her love. She was the answer to his fears, as the heavens were very well aware that fire could not be domesticated. However, an equilibrium for both was equally as destructive, for she was ice that melted at his touch. The universe had a sadistic sense of humor. He was to teach her how to feel, and she was to teach him how to heal. That was their only purpose.

Forgive me for what I do, as I do it on purpose. Be patient for there is method to my madness. I feed your conscience, but starve your existence. My angels and saints have danced with yours, but my devils and demons flourish in fires alone. I do not thirst for the warmth between the pillars of your being. I crave the awakening of their passionate fires of hell, so I can immerge fire with fire to be one with your soul.

Perhaps what I loved most about her was that when she was with me, she wore facades of frailties all mine to protect like she needed me. The truth was that she had no clue that I knew of the illusion she put on for me. She was the strongest, most independent woman I had ever known, and in my absence she was a warrior. I found peace in knowing she was safe whenever I wasn't there, no matter how much she claimed to have needed me. My little lady carried herself like a boss, and indeed a boss she was.

I often found myself drifting in and out of consciousness, falling asleep to the tranquility in her voice. I had never felt being so much at peace than when I was close to her. There was a strange sense of serenity in her presence that my storms would succumb to. She was the peace of mind I had always prayed for and had been without for so long.

Dolled up, she was the most confident version of herself. But I wished to convince her to be most comfortable in her own skin for all that she was. Whenever I caught her without her makeup, I looked at her as if I had fallen in love with her all over again. All I wanted was for her to believe I loved her for the perfectly put in place imperfections. Every time she blushed, I was certain that she came closer to believing that she was absolutely gorgeous without the aid of contour and layers of beautiful lies. I just wished for her to see herself through my eyes, so I wouldn't have to remind her as often; indeed she was a doll.

She always dreamt of a prince to take her away, and I was nothing but an ordinary man. She deserved to be in a palace, while the shores washed away my castles made of sand. But no prince would look at her the way I would, as if she's all that exists. For her I would build and empire, even if it meant being a slave to earn all its bricks.

I know
you have
been played
enough
to be
tired of
trying;

may
what is
yours
fall into
place
without
the need
for games.

-    a note to the reader

My heart whispers at the sight of you,
"There it is... My entire Kingdom."

Maybe one day we'll
sit hand in hand by the
fireplace and look back
at all the times we thought
we'd never be.

Perhaps one day
we will fight over
who loves the other more.

It is a war I swear
to never let you win.

I still remember the first time I called her my Queen. She refused to accept it, insisting that she was the King. I didn't let her win the argument though because she was still settling for less. I knew one day I'd tell her, she's my entire Kingdom.

It is in between the spaces
of her fingers, where I reside;

for the thought of her hands
in mine brings me home.

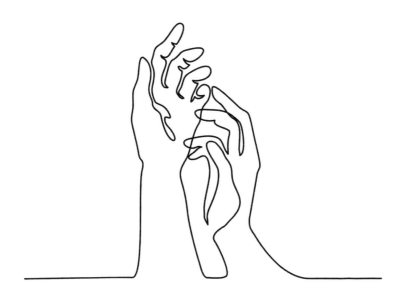

Everyone signifies the
end of the world with
asteroids falling from the sky.

To me, the world falling apart
is no less than a single tear
falling from her eyes.

They asked me what
the meaning of life was,
I gave them your name.

They clarified asking
for my purpose,
I told them no matter
how they phrase the question,
my answer will always be the same.

My soul knows yours like the ocean knows its depths, for there is nothing more to me than you. I am unaware of you being molded out of my rib, or if you are another soul altogether pulled from my own. Nor am I sure if I belong to you, or if it is the other way around. All I'm sure of is that you and I are no coincidence; for you are the key and the hereafter is home.

I don't know if these are what you call butterflies or if it's a hurricane swirling in my chest, but whatever it is... You've got my heart racing in ways only you know how. There is a certain madness to the way I feel. Could it possibly be called anything else, other than love?

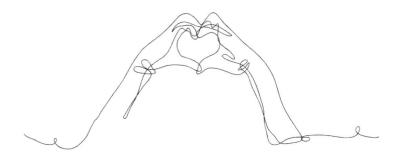

When you find yourself alone and worried, do you feel a tingle above your brows, as if it aches for something missing? Forgive me if that sounds awkward, but I wonder if you've felt all the times I've wanted to kiss your forehead and tell you that you'll be okay.

I really hope I make
you smile as often as
I think I do.

I just wish I could
always be there to
see it as often as I want to.

There are certain things
that we never get used to,

and they continue to mean
as much to us even after a
thousand times over.

Everything about you is
as special as it was the first time.

I wonder what territories
the tip of my tongue will
conquer for you to realize
how much of you is mine.

Out of all the thoughts
that weigh me down,
the possibility of ever
losing you torments me
the most.

Nothing made me more
uncomfortable than silence,

until I realized I could share
it with you.

Her nails clawed to his back.
His bite marks on her thighs.

The battle scars spoke for themselves,
what more to love was there other than war?

If I were asked to label the relationship between us, there would be no words to symbolize the chaos between her and I. It was more of an intense nympholepsy between our angels and demons, where parts of her yearned to save me while parts of me longed to destroy her.

Try
not to
be in it
too deep
for someone
who hasn't
even soaked
their foot
into the
shallow
end.

- a note to the reader

There are people you fall in love with, there are people you grow into loving, and then there are those you've always loved without ever knowing it. The latter is the kind of love that isn't learned nor acquired; the kind that was always there but had been dependent on a second encounter. The kind my soul feels for you, like it had already known you from another time and place.

I used to adore listening to music until every verse became about you. The idea of hearing your praise from a voice other than my own enraged me. Is it so bad that I cannot tolerate even the thought of another being in love with you?

She found it surprising that I admired everything she thought to hide from me. For example, she made sure to hide her face whenever she had no make up on, and that's when I made sure to tell her she looked the most beautiful. She always shied away, and I forced her to look me in the eyes when I said it, so she knew I meant it. Whenever she was on the verge of emotional chaos, she pushed me away so I don't see that side of her, and that's when I made sure to tell her she was the strongest woman I had ever met. Every time I touched her, was to make her feel comfortable in her own skin. She claimed to have flaws, but the only thing I saw was something to love. Loving her otherwise would have meant to be in love with the idea of her. But I made sure to convince her that she wasn't a figment of my imagination, but the closest thing to reality I had ever known. I knew what I had was perfect, and she didn't need filters to prove it.

It was inevitable; shots were fired. There was no point in trying to avoid the unavoidable. The sounds of warfare echoed across the battlefield. For the first few minutes it was utter chaos with an exchange between the heavy artillery on both sides. It wasn't the first time I had been behind enemy lines, and although I had enough ammunition to last me the entire war, the look in the enemy's eyes was intoxicating enough to arouse a ceasefire on my end. As always, I was caught off guard by the fury in her gaze. It no longer concerned me if she laid down her weapons or not. She was beyond beautiful when she'd get angry. Was it trance or tranquility? I could never figure it out! Everything went into slow motion, and I could even hear my heart pounding in my chest as if she went on a rampage against it. She was a massacre in disguise, the kind that'd seduce you to your own demise. Love is the only war in which you sleep with the enemy, and I signed up to be a martyr.

Every
time she
was caressed
by the
jaws of death,

she
had in
fact never
felt safer.

She
was in
love with
a lion,

and
she knew
he'd rip
the world
apart for
her.

Perhaps what troubled me most was how easily I convinced her that I loved her, when in fact I didn't. In all honesty, I felt nowhere close to it. Every time she smiled, I kissed her and she never saw through me. It tormented my soul every time I told her and she believed it, and yet I lied to her every single day. I gave her comfort in lies and nothing else made me as uncomfortable as continually doing it, but I continued to lie to her because I didn't know any other way. She found solace in the sweetest of my lies. If only she could have known how the truth was far sweeter, for what I felt for her was stronger than love. It'd make love seem like a joke. Truth is, there was no word for the way I felt. Telling her I loved her was like calling murder a paper cut, for it killed me on the inside thinking she'll never know the true essence of exactly how much she meant to me. So I continued lying to her, hoping that one day the truth would fend for itself.

As much as the territorial beast in me wants to rip your clothes off and bite into your skin to claim your entirety as mine; as much as it craves caressing your back dimples while carving its finger nails onto your waist line and leaving definitive claw marks down your spine – the faith that I hold on to has taught me to tame its intimately carnivorous demons. However, I am after all as man as any, and thus I will leave my mark. One so apparent that you will be forced to show it, for anyone aware of the fire between you and I will know that the smile you wear, and the confidence you flaunt is a mark of the love that no man other than myself could have left on you. Judge me then for the woman I made you into while respecting everything womanly about you, for if my demons can allow as much... imagine what kind of woman the fulfillment of my sainthood could have made you become.

and
then
my
world
turned
upside
down.

Some days it was perfect, and on other days it made no sense to me at all. In the mornings I'd leave her as if I'd never seen her to be happier, and I'd come home to nights where she'd fall asleep pushing me away. Somewhere between all the, "I love yous," to the "I feel for yous", and "I honestly don't", to " I can't any more." I was torn away between reading her mind and trying to hold on to mine when I absolutely couldn't do either of it. I was never one to give up too soon, but it was the confusion that eventually broke me. Being numb was the only thing that worked, and I eventually learned how not to feel at all. Even that was a lie I told myself, hoping one day I'll actually believe it.

Somewhere between
losing the you I used to know,

and becoming acquainted
with the new you,

I still looked for the
old you in all the things
that changed.

Perhaps I wasn't sure of what to do or where to go from where we stood. As much as it was a torment to my heart, mind, and soul, I let it get the best of me as if I had given her an open invitation to come and destroy me as she willed. I let her take me in circles, giving her the side of me that felt like hers even when I wasn't hers anymore. As much as it ripped me apart, I stood there making sure she was all in one piece. She was used to me, and I became a toy for her to ease out of no matter what it did to me. All I wanted was to be the one guy at whom she'd look back to and think, "He wasn't like the rest of them." What I wanted was to prove that we are not all the same.

I stand
on the
shores of
solitude,

waiting
for the
tide to
come in.

I would
drown
in its
wrath,

just to
hide the
state of
mind that
I'm in.

Some feel to the point
where it consumes them.
Others feel to the point
where it numbs them.
I just hope whatever you
feel is enough for who you
feel for without having to be empty.

- a note to the reader

They say death comes
to you once,

but through watching
you slowly slip away,

every step of it was
a death in itself.

Georgette is the fabric of my heart, and its torment is that of it being pulled across a bed of nails. Each thread ripped apart ruthlessly in the efforts of simply wanting to do what it was made to do. In trying to love, all it did was fail to be loved in return.

You'll always find a way out when you're looking for one, no matter how many doors I close to keep you safe. I can fight the world reaching in for you, but not the longing to leave that is inside of you.

Somewhere between
what actually was,

and what was meant
to be is nothing but
two hearts torn between
what could have been;

where nothing to one
was the other's everything.

I am still trying to figure
out what to do when you
go from being a priority
to being made to feel as
if you don't exist anymore.

Go ahead and belittle me
by saying what I feel for
you will soon be replaced
for someone else.

One day, time will attest
that it took for the end of
it to relieve me of the ache
that I carry within my chest.

All I ever wanted
was to love you like
you'll never be loved
the same.

So that whenever they
speak of love,

you'll always whisper
my name.

 Instagram: @ArslanWrites

With
time you
became
so much
of me,

that
I am
no longer
myself
without
you.

You can play oblivious to it now, but one day you'll find her in the reflection of every shiny surface, every dark window and mirror you walk across. You'll find her in your shadow, you'll hear her when you laugh, her voice will echo when you speak. I'll love you the point of madness, where you'll forget who you were before I walked into your life. It'll become second nature to you, that when you go out looking for yourself, all you'll ever find is the girl I love.

Every now and then we get distracted and we run into someone exhibiting bits and pieces of what we are looking for. In getting comfortable, we let those bits and pieces grow on us. Don't settle and don't let those bits and pieces grow in on you. You're meant for something whole that is made to synchronize with you flawlessly. Don't try to make the wrong pieces fit, because you are meant for more than just bits and pieces to be mixed and matched with yours. You are a beautiful existence that holds a heart that is whole; meant to be loved as wholeheartedly.

- a note to the reader

If
you're
afraid of
losing
someone,

chances
are you've
already lost
them.

I realized that the
universe has a sense
of humour when I felt
with all I could,

only to learn that you
feel nothing at all.

How reckless is
one's own heart?

For it looks to break
at the hands of so many,

until it finds the right
one to fix it.

Instagram: @ArslanWrites

"We can't have it all,"
My heart aches at the thought of you.

I was a boost to your ego;
you were a blow to mine.

Who meant more to the other?
I still can't make up my mind.

Even chaos could be so beautiful;
try writing your name next to mine.

_____ Arslan

I've always had a thing for swords,
and she was my sharpest.

-   the slaughter

Perhaps it was destined
to be this way,
we all have a role to play.
I was meant to love you,
and your love was meant
to hurt one day.

Sometimes
the message
is sent,

but the
meaning is lost.

Eyes
so dry,

you
would
think
they're
thirsty.

The
depths
of what
they hide
will drown
you,

believe
me.

And then there are nights
you realize breathing has
very little do to with being alive.

In the battlefield of love,
it is often pride that prevailed.

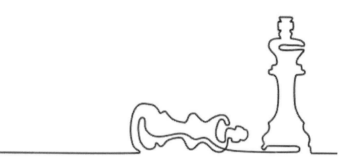

She was the author to the perfect heartbreak. I let her go in circles to write me into a series of page-turners, sequel after sequel with secrets I'd take to my grave. For there are two types of writers: the kinds that immortalize you on paper, and the ones like her who kill you with scar-like pen strokes on your heart that bleed prose internally for no one else to see.

Instagram: @ArslanWrites

I close these eyes of mine only to be haunted by flashbacks of the times I spent looking into yours. I stay awake not because of insomnia or the inability to fall asleep right away, but because even in my dreams I can no longer seem to find the same comfort in your eyes that I once took for granted. I'd rather torture myself being awake than to fall asleep and be haunted by the very person I once called home, not being able to recognize me anymore.

There was so much of what was mine I could find in just a glimpse into your eyes, but now I find nothing but the same loneliness that I'm surrounded by in being without you. It's as if I left you so stranded that a part of your emptiness haunts me in return for the voids that I've left you with.

In all the people you have yet to lose, a part of yourself will be lost with them, as you've lost parts of yourself in whomever else before that never made it through. So choose wisely of whom you invest yourself in. It happens ever so often that you are left with a version of yourself that you no longer recognize anymore. That is the person who is hardest to live with, and ironically enough that is whom you'll never seem to lose again.

- a note to the reader

The decision of fate was a divine intervention for our demons to steer clear of one another, as we shared an intimacy even the angels envied. The union of you and I was chaos, enough for all hell to break loose in the heavens above.

It's when I try to numb myself to it, that I feel it the most. Piercing through deeper and deeper into the layers of my heavily guarded realm of hope, wanting me to give in to it as if I have no choice but to break. At times, I'm caught off guard and it comes to me when I least expect it and my fight against my hurt humiliates me excruciatingly. Eventually you became the heaviness that I feel pulsating between my breaths, as if your name was enough for my heart to sink at the thought of there being nothing left. I'll learn to live with it though, as heavy as it gets… I'll carry it.

May you find it
within yourself to heal,

for what is written for you
deserves you whole.

- a note to the reader

Your silence is a storm in itself.
You don't need words to destroy me.

I'm entangled in thoughts
of the dreams I could have
seen during the nights I didn't sleep.

Inquisitive of all that could
have came true if I hadn't
invested my peace of mind in you.

All this heart really
wants is someone to
live for and to never
go a day without being
wanted in return.

So often that becomes
too little and perhaps
too much at the same time.

Perhaps it's not about
falling for the wrong person.
It's about falling too selflessly
for the right person that
inevitably pushes them into
becoming wrong for you.

- attempts at making sense
  of all that fails to make any
  sense at all.

I guess I got so used to
being neglected and ignored,
that when I finally have
your attention,

I don't even know what
to do with it anymore.

- insecurity

The ache in my heart
is one that I can no
longer put into words,
and that in itself is an
ache of its own.

Perhaps it wasn't that
you could never be enough,
but that you were too much
for someone destined for too little.

- denial

Sometimes death feels
like the only cure to the
ache in your heart;

But learning to live with
the pain is making an ordinary
life into a work of art.

- a note to the reader

Had I known I was among options for you to choose from, I would have let go of you the moment you made it clear. I would fight the world for you, but I would never compete. I am a conqueror; I take what I believe to be mine; not a competitor to have you settle for me.

Everything about you was so right,
except for the fact that you were wrong;
and that is something I am still trying
to wrap my head around.

... but perhaps the togetherness of two equally broken souls is still not equivalent to the predestined fit of the two halves of a single whole already written for us. Maybe that is why the universe has a way of conspiring against people like you and I. It seems to favor the choice of fate against accidents of luck, such as how the crossing of paths between us shall soon become of irrelevance. You'll let go eventually and I'll have to move on. You'll lose yourself to someone else, but the end of you and I individually will never be the same love again. We may fall one day, but it will never be exactly this. What I know for sure is that in the heavens they'll speak of us as a beautiful misfortune that could never be fortunate enough for fate to change its mind.

The ghost of yesterdays past kept haunting me in every day that turned today; flashbacks to holding her in my arms whenever I saw her walk by. I could still feel the warmth of her skin against mine. What I once called home was now a distant memory that still called out to me, but couldn't be bothered with me in reality. I couldn't look her in the eyes the same. Every thing was a reminder of the territory I once marked. Her lips once caressed mine, her hands once firmly held on to mine, her voice once called out to me like the perfect chorus to a beautiful song still on my mind. She was the biblical scripture that enlightened me. Her body was a crusade that I once fought. Her beautiful mind made me into a missionary that preached what she thought. How do I abandon that?

Instagram: @ArslanWrites

In the coldest of nights I yearned for her. She was the sun that melted my ice-cold bitterness away. She was the rain that rejuvenated the valves of my heart, almost like branches to a tree brought back to life it seemed. She was like spring; she healed all that was left destroyed in the winter past. She was the wind that blew away the dried up leaves of sorrows in my mind. She was the cure to the drought inside me; that thirsts to feel again. She brought to life what was known to have died within me. She was simply a breath of fresh air; her presence gave me life. I realized in her absence that I had only been existing. It was her that made me feel alive.

If it were up to me,
I'd shade you from
even the rays of the sun.

But it is a torment in itself
knowing that I will never be the one.

Out of all the things that I lost, I never found the one I was meant to hold on to. Being on the verge of losing myself entirely, all I needed now was someone to have faith in the parts of me that I had given up on. I needed someone to stand with me, and not just beside me. But that's how it is sometimes. What is meant to be yours eventually finds you a little too late.

Even though the complexities of life had made it clear that she was the half to another whole, I tried to hold on to her as if she was the only piece I could ever imagine penetrating through my soul. Such is the tragedy of the heart, for when it dedicates itself to the one it sees fit, no one could ever fulfill it, or play the role of whom it beats for.

I guess I wasn't meant to stop for you, and you were meant to look the other way. Our eyes were never meant to meet as such, and our stars would never have aligned this way. You were never to have fallen, and I wouldn't have had to catch you with open arms. I was never meant to feel for you, and you were never to have known what it means to be loved as such. You never should have heard my voice, and I wasn't supposed to make you laugh. I was never to have pulled you close, and you were never meant to submit to me. Never should have all these wrongs felt so right, but nothing has ever made sense this way. Perhaps all the wrongs were meant to be, and we were meant to leave our mark. Maybe you and I had to meet and soon depart, so we'd know whom to look for in the world hereafter.

Even though you are no longer mine, I am forever confined to long for the parts of myself that I left with you, that you haven't even held on to. I guess I haven't gotten used to accepting that a part of me was also lost in the process of losing you.

Instagram: @ArslanWrites

Fate was the ultimate slayer of the dragons that love had awoken within the two of us. Had we indulged in the rituals of breathing fire, it would have been enough to destroy the both of us. Just as a taste of the warmth of your flames had me rapt in wonder, imagine what euphoria the complete carnal conquest of your existence would have induced. We were drowning in sin, unconsciously wanting to be saved and here we are now... Trying to adjust to changes neither of us would admit to have prayed for in the midst of finding serenity in our own destruction.

May what you chase after
stops for a moment and
accepts all that you are,

for ever so often our
desires repel us ever
so instinctively.

You deserve far more
than to be on the receiving
end of that.

-   a note to the reader

I finally understand that
I can not attach myself to
a soul not meant for me,

for one who is meant to be
with another will never find
peace in my company

The world comes to an
end every time the thought
of you comes to mind.

I have scars and bruises
from all the things that
failed to hurt me,

and yet I have nothing
to show for the love that
nearly destroyed me.

I have fought battles
both external and
within myself,

but sharing you with
anyone else has by far
been the hardest.

How
unfair
is it to
be made
to feel
all over
again,

all
that you
taught
yourself
not to
feel?

I owe the ache
in my heart to
the irony of fate,

I fell for poison ivy,
dressed in floral prints.

If only it was as easy
to fall out of the mess
you let yourself fall into.

You have no idea how
high I would go just to
fall out of love with you.

and
that
is
how
the
butterflies
in
my
stomach,
ended
up
becoming
flames
in
my
heart.

I should have let you go a long time ago, for it was only after I did was it that I finally learned what it meant to be free. I've been at peace since, and it is beyond me how I could have ever associated it with you.

My love validated
your existence for
far too long,

that it came to a point
where I began to question
my own.

I have become far too cruel to wish death upon my enemy, for that'd kill him too soon. I believe in a slow and painful type of death, the kind that unreciprocated love puts you through.

-   things I don't really mean

Out of all the things that I hate,
I loved you the most.

I wouldn't wish on an enemy…
a love like yours.

and
one
day
you
find
peace.

Life is merely a puppet show. We are all dancing at the hands of fate, constantly tangling and untangling amongst one another. Some of us accidentally end up in knots until fate decides to unwind them, whereas others were meant to be tied together to begin with. Do not be hung over a knot that was untangled for you, because at the right point in time, your strings will intertwine with the right set of strings for you to fall into the perfect mess of knots that no power can unwind. Until then... dance at the hands of the Puppet Master pulling the strings. The stage is His, and He knows exactly what He's doing.

- a game of strings

... and some day which may come sooner than you know it, the part of you that died will have found peace and will have moved on. It will carry your sorrows, your grief, and all the reasons you disbelieved, to a destination far beyond your reach. You see, in order to be whole again, you need to be torn apart. You will be put back together in all the right ways into the masterpiece that you are meant to become, but for that to happen, you must break in all the right pieces from all the right places. When it's all said and done, all that will be left behind are faded memories of what made you weak, only to have inevitably made you stronger. The workings of life are beyond our control, but the One in control of life itself knows exactly the extent of which you can withstand. Let His Supreme Deity help you grow into what He needs you to become. Your purpose is written, and your struggles will only prepare you for the fulfillment of that purpose. Train well. Some day you'll understand what every trial you withstood had been preparing you for. Till then, bend until you break. Your reconstruction awaits you.

This seems like the end,
but it is only the beginning.
May what finds you next,
erase all the hurt from the past.
May you love and be loved,
like never before.

-    Arslan Zaidi

Printed in Great Britain
by Amazon